I0198843

Preface

One of my most vivid childhood memories has to do with *Frankenstein*, specifically Frankenstein's monster. My brother had received a plastic model kit of the monster for his birthday. My brother was, I don't know, eight or nine, and if so I was five or six. Our father, who never said much about his childhood, told us that he was terrified of Frankenstein's monster when he was a kid. He'd seen the movie (I assume it was the 1931 James Whale-directed version), and the image of the monster affected him for months. The model (the kind that you glue together and paint) was *modeled* after Boris Karloff. Many years later, in the mid-80s, I would read Mary Shelley's novel for the first time, and discover that her vision of the creature was quite different from the better-known one that James Whale gave us in his iconic film.

Upon neither encounter (in the 60s and the 80s) did I have any idea how influential Mary Shelley's work would be in my own creative interests. In 1998 I took a job that afforded me the opportunity to teach *Frankenstein*, and I would continue to do so for the next twenty-five years. Details of Mary Shelley's life as well as the complexities of her most famous novel thoroughly soaked into my psyche. In the early 2000s I wrote a short story, "A Wintering Place," that was a sequel to *Frankenstein*, focusing on the creature beyond the scope of the novel. The story was published in the literary journal *Eleven Eleven* (I've since reprinted it twice, including in *Delta of Cassiopeia: Collected Stories and Sonnets* [2023]). Later I wrote the novel *An Untimely Frost* (2014), which was inspired by the fact that Mary Shelley (widowed) and Washington Irving (living in London) entertained the idea of a romantic relationship—a relationship that never materialized, except in my novel. Then I wrote the novel *Mrs Saville* as a sequel to *Frankenstein* (published in 2018 to coincide with the bicentennial of Mary Shelley's book).

I've listed here my work that has been *directly* influenced by *Frankenstein* and by Mary Shelley herself, but I have no doubt their *indirect* influences can be found throughout my oeuvre.

Although I write in many modes, I think of myself mainly as a novelist. However, between 2016 and 2021 I wrote a series of sonnets to my late father. It was a way to speak to him and to consider our relationship, after his sudden passing in 2012. By the conclusion of 2024 I was in the mood to write more sonnets, but I no longer felt the need to write to my father. So throughout the holidays I considered various subjects for my sonneteering. It struck me that a literary subject could prove fruitful. Again I considered options. The question lingered in the back of my consciousness—until I had a Eureka moment (or a Joycean epiphany): Mary Shelley. I would write some sonnets to Mary Shelley.

I began writing my sonnets in apostrophe to Mary W. Shelley on January 7, 2025 (according to my sonnet notebook). At first I thought I would write a handful of sonnets, just enough to scratch the itch and have some poems to circulate for publication, before returning to work on a novel project. However, I found the subject matter to be exceptionally rich, and the process to be exceptionally enjoyable. Consequently the project grew from a constellation of sonnets to enough for a chapbook and finally to enough for a collection. Ultimately, over the course of about six months, I wrote 103 sonnets (I cut three from the collection for one reason or another). Early on I decided I would bracket the collection between Mary Godwin's birth (1797) and Mary Shelley's return to London after spending five years in Italy (1823).

Her most significant literary achievement from the period

Also by Ted Morrissey

Fiction
The Strophes of Job
Delta of Cassiopeia
First Kings and Other Stories
The Artist Spoke
Mrs Saville
The Curvatures of Hurt
Crowsong for the Stricken
Weeping with an Ancient God
An Untimely Frost
Figures in Blue
Men of Winter

Scholarship
"Vox Humana": A Casebook (with Amina Ghazanfar)
A Concise Summary and Analysis of The Mueller Report
Trauma Theory as a Method for Understanding Literary Texts
The *Beowulf* Poet and His Real Monsters

Aspiring Child

Aspiring Child

A Biography of
Mary W. Shelley
in Sonnets

Ted Morrissey

TWELVE WINTERS
a literary project

Published by Twelve Winters, a literary project.

P. O. Box 414 • Sherman, Illinois 62684-0414 • twelvewinters.com

Aspiring Child was first published by Twelve Winters in 2026. All rights reserved.

ISBN
979-8-9933215-0-9

Printed in the United States of America

For Mary—
& all the Marys
(And for Melissa, always)

Acknowlegments

With much appreciation to the editors of journals where many of these sonnets first appeared, at times in somewhat different form: *The Basilisk Tree, The Brussels Review, Disturbances, Feminist Spaces, HAUNTER Review, The Poetry Lighthouse, Rockvale Review,* and *The Soliloquist.*

It would be impossible to cite all the sources that contributed to the writing of this book, but I would be remiss in not naming at least two: *The Monsters: Mary Shelley and the Curse of Frankenstein* by Dorothy and Thomas Hoobler; and the work of scholar, author and documentarian Sir Christopher Frayling.

— T. M.

Sequence

Continued

Note: Various texts are *quoted* in the sonnets—letters, diaries, reviews, books, etc.—and the borrowings appear in italics rather than quotation marks, in part because at times they are not verbatim. Due to poetic considerations they may be lightly edited, but never to the point of altering their meaning.

was of course *Frankenstein*, but I didn't want this collection to be solely about the conceiving of and the writing of that watershed book. Mary Wollstonecraft Shelley was so much more than "the author of *Frankenstein*," and I hope *Aspiring Child* provides a more panoramic view of an extraordinary woman who led an extraordinary (and at times extraordinarily difficult) life.

T. M.

Sherman, Illinois

September 29, 2025

They say that thou wert lovely from thy birth,
Of glorious parents, thou aspiring child.
— Percy Bysshe Shelley, LAON AND CYTHNA

In an instant I dared to shake off my chains, and look around me
with a free and lofty spirit; but the iron had eaten into my flesh,
and I sank again, trembling and hopeless, into my miserable self.
— Mary W. Shelley, FRANKENSTEIN

Aspiring Child

I

Your mother left you, eleven days old.
Taken away by her newest lover,
Death. Septic poisoning, likely from
the doctor's dirty nails as he groped
for her obstinate placenta. You always
felt responsible, a lonely little girl
burdened with that and a clever mind
out of time. Your name echoed her absence.
But she bequeathed you her books,
her revolutionary spirit, the vindication
of your alienated rights. Her words
worked to fill the emptiness, the void,
as you grew and read and waited, aching
for a dangerous affair of your own.

Vindication

II

It was only paint, darkness and light—
her portrait above the bare mantel,
animated by her books, words on a
page, darkness and white, and by
the stories your widowed father
would tell when his new wife wasn't
near. The public did its worst to muck
her memory (a radical woman; unwed).
You sought her like spirit graveside,
St. Pancras, place of solace. Proud
whenever someone remarked how
much you resembled her. You knew:
you did, more than they could know.
Both her darkness and her light.

St. Pancras

5

III

Did your father love you? Or was he
simply determined to do his paternal
duty, be true to his own philosophy
of childrearing and liberal pedagogy?
Dedicated to his sense of himself more
than to you—the daughter whose life
claimed that of his wife, his soul mate.
Death the midwife at your bloody birth.
Were they symbols of his affection:
the public lectures, the ceaseless lessons,
the adult-size erudition? Unchecked access
to a world-class library in his unmistakably
middle-class home? As unmistakable as
your destiny to follow his path (and hers).

Devotion

6

IV

Stepmother tensions sent you to Dundee
at fourteen. The Baxters and their
daughters were welcoming, as were the
cold and damp Scottish docks, where
cosmopolitan traffic traded stories
more valuable to you than other exotic
commodities. Your clever mind was
enflamed like a Promethean torch.
You dreamed of a daring sea captain
marooned in an arctic waste as
vast as your imagination. A doting
sister waited and worried back in
London—as you wished your dear
father did without his only daughter.

Marooned

V

In your book's oft-quoted 1831 introduction
you give the impression that you grew up
in the wilds of Scotland, a place that trained
your fancy to run free, a catalyst to your
burgeoning creativity. But most of your life,
before you met Shelley, was in London,
at the overcrowded and confining Skinner
Street house, close to St. Pancras cemetery.
You present an image we may associate
with the Brontës upon their rainswept moors.
My habitual residence was on the blank
and dreary northern shores of the Tay, or
the bleak sides of the woodless mountains.
We understand rewriting one's childhood.

Revision

VI

Maybe the lightness, the freedom you
felt in Scotland—the live-in friend of
Christy Baxter—wasn't simply a matter
of shedding stepmother tensions on
Skinner Street. Perhaps in Dundee
you could be someone other than
Mary Wollstonecraft's daughter. Her
reputation followed you everywhere.
It must've seemed that all of London
watched for signs and symptoms
of your own inevitable downfall.
How far, they wondered, had the
apple fallen from the maternal tree?
How soon will the fruit prove rotten?

Anticipation

VII

You found him there, on your visit home.
Unearthly, brilliant, charming, educated,
as devoted to your parents' ideas as you.
But married and a father at twenty-one.
Poet, freethinker, an acolyte in your
father's circle. It must have been a brief
encounter but one imagines you sensed
all that was to come: the losses, the pain.
The future a shade, a shadow, a presence
like the past that always lingered near.
Or maybe in him you saw an end to
the loneliness, the longing—you had never
met the stranger, happiness, so how
could you reliably recognize him now?

Acolyte

VIII

The atheist, Percy Bysshe Shelley,
called on your father, one of his heroes,
and found a trinity of possibilities. He
liked teenage girls in need of saving,
and there you all were at Skinner Street:
Fanny, Claire and you—probably all
interested and ready to respond to
his blue-eyed overtures of affection.
But you stood apart, still dressed in
the tartans of your adopted Scotland,
the very image of your dead mother,
whom Percy may have already loved,
that is, the vivid persona enlivened
by the radical writings in her books.

Trinity

IX

Your letters expressed a breathless
excitement at the plan to escape,
and anxiousness that the debt-collectors
would catch him before you could cross
the channel. And they emphasized your
eternal devotion, which may have seemed
a juvenile sheen but time proved you true.
Your own Mary who loves you so tenderly.
Yours would not be an easy pairing.
There would be a plague of problems:
finances always, his faithlessness, family,
his, yours—and the unvaried visitations
of Death. But there remained the words,
the work, the memory to immortalize.

Escape

X

You were chattel, said the scandalmongers,
sold to the baronet, you and your stepsister,
to buttress your father's frail finances. Not
true of course, and he was angry in his
embarrassment at your impulsive elopement
to the Continent—not in practice the radical
he had always painted himself in print.
Your appeals did nothing to appease him.
Shelley meanwhile seemed impervious to
the stabs of hurtful gossip—of course *he*
could be—*he* had that luxury. You inspired
comparisons to your scandalous mother,
whose circumstances the cruel wags
had neither forgotten nor forgiven.

Gossip

XI

Your escape to the Continent ended
when you ran out of money. The three
of you, defeated and deflated, drifted
home along the Rhine via noisy public
barge. The scenery compensated for
the uncouth company: sharply climbing
hills and crumbling castles—ideal images
for your somber Romantic sensibilities.
At Gernsheim, you and Shelley went on
a three-hour ramble. Within imposing
view was *the castle of the Franks* with
its legend of the alchemist who mixed
human blood with animal bones in search
of the elixir of life. Herr Frankensteiner.

Transport

XII

1814-1815. Back in London. Persecuted,
poor and pregnant. You had fallen as far
as your mother, said public sentiment.
Percy introduced you to his friend Hogg,
hoping you two would fall in love. He may
feel remorse that he chose you over Claire,
and your stepsister seems open to the idea.
Likely Percy would prefer to have you both.
A lifeline arrived in the death of Sir Bysshe,
Percy's grandfather: £1,000 per annum.
The wolf driven somewhat from the door,
you prepared for the arrival of your first
child, depending mostly on Hogg for your
emotional support. You were seventeen.

Wolves

XIII

You were intimately familiar with all your
mother's work but were especially drawn
to her Scandinavian *Letters*, published
the year before your birth. The hybrid text
(which foreshadowed a book like *Moby
Dick*, which itself foreshadowed high
modernism) no doubt informed the writing
of your book, in its structure, its scope.
But it was your mother's persona in the
Letters that inspired such strong empathy.
Against the rugged backdrop, one senses
her loneliness, her simple sadness at having
been dismissed, forsaken by those she loved.
Only able to depend on her wits, her resolve.

Sweden

XIV

Claire set out to catch a poet of her own—
why not the most famous (and *most
dangerous*), Lord Byron? Your stepsister
was seventeen when she began writing
to the notorious libertine, asserting her
devotion . . . and eager availability. She
used your notoriety and literary pedigree
as enticement for an in-person audience.
Public scrutiny had become too intense
(and creditors too aggressive) so Byron
planned to abscond to Geneva. Claire
pressured him for the address, keeping
her intentions and her condition a secret.
You had long admired Byron's poetry.

Hunting

XV

In your journal there's no mention of help
with the birth of your daughter who died
nameless at twelve days. No nurse, no
maid, no one. Your stepsister's task was
to distract the high-strung Percy, it seems.
You were seventeen. Your mother's death,
due to *your* birth, must have lain like lead.
A presence like a phantasmagoric midwife.
No wonder, then, that Victor is so utterly
alone when he *infuses a spark of being
into the lifeless thing on a dreary night
in November.* Henry Clerval arrives just
when Victor needs his loving support.
Your stepmother sent clean linen.

Arrival

XVI

Shelley: *the child not expected to live.*
Born at seven months, she had little
chance of survival. Still, you cared for
her, bonded with her. March 5: *Nursed
my baby.* March 6: *Find my baby dead.*
You couldn't stop thinking about the
little girl who didn't live long enough to
be named. Just twelve troubled days.
She haunted your sleep: *Dreamt that
it had only been cold & we rubbed it
by the fire & it lived—I wake and find
no baby.* Only Ovid could distract your
grieving: tales of transformations, of
living again beyond one's tragic death.

Metamorphosis

XVII

The elopement was a kind of examination—
an immersion in great books and pillow-talk
discussions, followed by a test for matriculation:
a literary achievement worthy of your famous
parents, evidence of your mother's mettle,
your father's mental acuity. Goethe, Rousseau,
Milton, Coleridge; then sequestered with Byron,
Shelley, their idols, and their Romantic ideals.
War-ravaged Europe was your classroom.
The war-damaged Continent your curriculum.
You ran this pedagogical gauntlet, this trial-
by-thought, while also learning how to care
for your new son, named for your silent father:
a silence more terrible than your dead mother's.

Matriculation

XVIII

They waited impatiently, mainly for you to fail:
Who were you to compete with the poets,
who would no doubt find writing a ghost
story simple child's play? Embarrassed,
mortified (still traumatized by the loss of your
baby), you must acknowledge each morning
you had thought of no story, one imagines
much to their smug and preening satisfaction.
Then came the nightmare of *the pale student
of unhallowed arts lying beside the thing.* You,
a terrorized girl, had witnessed with closed eyes
the birth of a myth, more potent than Prometheus.
Something new to haunt you, this hideous phantom.
Beyond the shutters, the Alps shivered in moonlight.

Myth

XIX

A memory: You hid behind the parlor couch
so that you could hear the great man recite
his great poem. The tale within a tale. The
harassed mariner driven to the icy wastes
of the southern pole. His companions
risen from the dead. The punishment of
unabated guilt—a feeling familiar to you
on that fateful night. You were only eight.
Ten summers later its images of ice
and death and crushing guilt would grow
into your own great work. In your interwoven
tales the mariner himself would arise now
and again, still harassed, still haunted,
still confessing his unforgivable sin.

Recitation

XX

The myth of Prometheus was a shared
preoccupation that famous summer: the
summer that wasn't. The summer of
storm and darkness. The summer of
grief. When nightmares waited patiently.
They embraced the Titan's suffering—
tormented for taking the gods' fire, for
aspiring to their divinity, their greatness.
You meanwhile enfolded a different version
of the story: Prometheus as creator of
man, as bestower of life—animating his
creation via his fiery breath. O to burn
with that power too beneath oppressive
clouds. Where nightmares waited quietly.

Creation

XXI

First on horseback, then by mule, finally
on foot you traversed the dangerous
Alpine path toward the imposing Mer de
Glace. *Nothing can be more desolate
than the ascent.* Rain and snow and ice
repelled your progress. Yet you managed
to reach the source of the Arveiron
surrounded by mountains and glaciers.
You would revisit this place of danger
and desolation, as would your readers,
a number beyond counting. The ice's
incessant advance, its cracking, its
falling *a foaming cataract.* The tumult,
the chaos that is prelude to creation.

Tumult

XXII

Polidori fancied you. The young doctor's
attentions and intentions were unmistakable,
that cold Genevan summer. Diodati was
your refuge from the raw weather. Claire
and Shelley sought Byron's company for
their own reasons. Polidori imagined himself
a man of letters also, eagerly accepting the
ghost-story challenge. He wrote of vampyres.
Perhaps he saw you as a victim, bled by
Shelley's wandering libido, baby William's
needs, Claire's needful clinging. He offered
himself as faithful friend, reliable partner:
medicine for Shelley's anemic love, while
rain wept across the villa's tall windows.

Anemia

XXIII

The great men would go for a sail on
Lake Geneva—alone with the wind and
the water and their great thoughts. You
remained behind at the villa, assuming
the responsibility of fair-copying Byron's
newest canto, the third. The poet's hero
has turned bitter and world-weary while
traveling across war-ravaged Europe.
Perhaps you saw it as a privilege, or
at least a rare opportunity. Another
component of your self-education.
Your unique mind separated the wheat
from the chaff, spinning it into a dark
story that would outshine them all.

Separation

XXIV

Beclouded Geneva, that cold summer:
metaphor for all the obscurity and
obfuscation. The secrets revealed in
private conversations, the confessions.
Leaving you to infer, to wonder, to worry.
Claire was pregnant (you guessed) but
by whom? She and Percy were always
whispering behind closed doors. Byron?
Secret machinations, tasks best done
in darkness, deals with the devil, acts
performed out of public view. Legal
documents drafted and signed. Secrecy
salted with shame flavored your writing,
slithered its way into your growing story.

Machinations

XXV

Phantasmagoria: you liked the word,
and the trick itself—creating spectral
images with glass and candlelight.
You and Shelly had seen a show two
years before Bryon read aloud the
book's title, while a storm cracked
and flashed, rattling Villa Diodati and
its impressionable young guests.
You may have been less spooked
than Shelley and the rest. After all
you'd lived alongside your mother's
spectre since birth and knew ghosts
to be comforting, even companionable.
You preferred haunting to abandonment.

Companions

XXVI

At Diodati, the men talked long into the
damp night: of the newest science, of
E. Darwin's experiments to imbue
animation, of Galvani and his powerful
battery. Your participation was not
encouraged, as the men suspected
your contributions would be irrelevant,
inconsequential, all in all unworthy.
You may have appeared blankly
disinterested as candlelight and
shadow played upon your young face.
Your mind, however, was its own sort
of powerful engine, fusing the ideas,
igniting electric sparks of imagination.

Introspection

XXVII

Byron had a midnight surprise: new poems
in manuscript from Coleridge, and one
was in keeping with the summer's vampiric
theme. Candlelight must have coruscated
along the Lord's firm jaw as he read
magnetically of Geraldine's terrifying
nipple-eyed breasts, sending Shelley
screaming from the drawing-room.
You must have wondered about your
bargain, an unmarried eighteen-year-old
with one baby in his bassinet and another
in her grave. You were learning that their
father was prone to his own infantile fits
. . . and succumbing to his selfish desires.

Terror

XXVIII

A notorious houseguest joined your Diodati
circle mid-August, a celebrity of the Gothic:
Matthew Lewis, author of *The Monk*, a tale
of secrecy, disguises, incest, and satanic oaths.
He shared his translation of Goethe's *Faust*.
Then one dark evening, candlelight quivering,
"Monk" Lewis recited five chilling ghost stories.
The air of mystery must have been marvelous.
None directly influenced your embryonic book—
but years later they would be the basis for the
essay *On Ghosts* in *London Magazine*, the
supernatural encounters culled from your
Genevan journal. The fruits of that unlikely
summer proved themselves cornucopian.

Guest

XXIX

You were experiencing your own sort of
expressionism that frigid summer, 1816.
The Swiss Alps cast a mood of foreboding
across the rain-soaked countryside, draped
as they were in indigo shadows and dreary
sunshine. The glacial lake was an icy bath
suited only for sailing amid the storm-
accelerated winds and accepting the dead.
But the relentless gloom suited you, fed
your depression, seeded your seething
imagination. The story you struggled to
write required such feelings: isolation,
devastation, impending doom. Your
alchemy turned the atmosphere into art.

Alchemy

XXX

Though it is not so simple, we like to say
two iconic monsters were born that stormy
night in Geneva—both popular beyond their
creators' expectations. Yet the monsters
are mirror images. Polidori's vampyre (a
portrait of Byron?) is attractive, magnetic:
a seductive aristocrat whose handsome
exterior conceals a purely malignant heart.
Your creation, however, is inherently good
but driven to monstrosity by the meanness
he elicits for being outwardly ugly. Later
symbolized in celluloid as villagers with
pitchforks and torches. Did you sense these
contrasts in the circle that enclosed you?

Contradiction

XXXI

How much of your book's complexity
was conscious? How much the product
of your unconscious mind's murky stew?
Your masterstroke—we see—was recasting
the Promethean ideal of risk-taking from
the realm of art to the realm of science.
An experiment in poetry run amok may
be an embarrassment, but a scientific risk . . .
Perhaps you perceived the difference
due to your and Shelley's social experiments:
the riskiness of free love, of espoused
atheism, of cohabitation without matrimony.
Monstrosities arisen from society's stewing
cauldron. Alienation pungent in the brew.

Risk

XXXII

From the start you imagined your ghost
story could be so much more than a thin
Gothic thriller—a book worthy of your
parents' weighty reputations. Despite
grief's leaden burden you embarked
on an ambitious course of research:
chemistry, geography, philosophy.
Meanwhile your world fell to pieces.
But trauma was your co-author and
every pen-stroke bled shades of pain:
abandonment, withheld love, lost hope.
Shelley complained of your coldness—
but you were alone, exploring your own
polar realm of darkness and desolation.

Exploration

XXXIII

The sun is forever visible—the belief of
your polar explorer, Walton. In spite
of the science, your contemporaries
wished it to be true: Beyond the untamed
seas, beyond the dangerous bergs,
the frozen pole became a restorative
paradise: Rich reward for navigating
the series of spirit-crushing obstacles.
Maybe like Captain Walton you held
onto a similar hope: Beyond the deaths,
beyond the ostracism, beyond the never-
ending worries, the world would transform
into a place of warmth. *What may not be
expected in a country of eternal light?*

Light

XXXIV

There are glimpses of domestic harmony
in your book: Victor's boyhood, the exiled
De Laceys. And there are hopes for such
happiness: Victor and Elizabeth's betrothal,
the creature with his manufactured mate
in the edenic jungles of South America.
But the fragile dynamics easily fracture,
the airy dreams always dissipate . . .
The Baxters, in Dundee, may have been
a tableau of tranquility, a truly happy
family. You spent the better part of two
years in their household, 1812-1814.
But you were always their guest, the
taste always tainted with impermanence.

Dissipation

XXXV

You compared literary production to the
chaos of creation—not something from
nothing, from a black void; but something
from countless sources. Just as Victor
stitched together his creation you wove
together yours. Drawing from everyone,
everything, everywhere: the materials
you must assemble like a manic surgeon.
Victor's ambition was beauty but he
achieved only monstrosity. What of your
creation? Critics have cataloged its
imperfections, its artistic slippages. But
there is no denying its monstrous power,
its penchant for survival and longevity.

Assembly

XXXVI

Those many months you toiled with your
book—simply *work* in your journal—a
favorite distraction was netting. To net
was to interlace and tie threads (to make
a garment, say). It is a perfect metaphor
for the complex structure of your novel,
the frames, the embedded voices, each
inside another—then every thread tied
together meticulously. Did the pastime
affect your writing, your plotting? Maybe
you were just attracted to complicated
entanglements. But could you avoid the
fates of Victor and Walton: to become
trapped in nets of their own making?

Structure

XXXVII

You were surrounded by atheists, both
the outspoken and the quiet (the camp
into which you fell). Your Romantic
companions sympathized with the devil:
a mascot of resistance to authority—
in whatever authoritative guise—
persecuted, punished for the failure
of allegiance, for thinking freely.
Your genetic myths came by way of
Milton, Satan's supreme advocate.
You placed your waning faith in Science,
though it proved as capricious as God.
At least Science offered no galling
pretenses of love and forgiveness.

Faith

40

XXXVIII

To Mrs. Saville, England—we are intro-
duced to Margaret Saville in the open-
ing line of your book: the intended
recipient of this long, strange epistle
composed by her brother, Walton.
She sits in an unpopulated narrative
realm with the potential for omniscience
if her brother's letter reaches her.
Long ago it was noticed that her initials,
M.S., are your own. Did you, too, sit
alone in London anxiously awaiting
omniscience, willing the substance
of your book to reach you somehow,
beating the obstacles and the odds?

Vessel

XXXIX

Yes, of course you were steeped in theories,
parenting and pedagogy, books by the most
progressive thinkers of the day, including
your own parents' treatises. They shaped
the story of your mistreated creature. Like
you, he was self-educated through reading,
close observation, social experimentation.
An imagination that was fired by isolation.
But your narrative wasn't solely formed by
your syllabus. The creature's loneliness is
also the loneliness of a little girl who spent
long hours by her mother's grave in intimate
communion but received only her silence.
The acute loneliness of maternal absence.

Absence

XL

Victor is an erratic father. At first a proud
parent marveling at his accomplishment;
then horrified by his creation as soon as
it begins to act independently. Later,
Victor softens and sees that he should
help his creature to be happy—only to
turn again, indifferent to his creation's
suffering, his loneliness, his misery.
You probably saw your father as this
same sort of maddeningly mercurial
parent. Inconsistent, unreliable. Able
to render you happy but just as likely
to deliver a devastating blow, a cutting
benediction of cruelty to lay you low.

Caprice

XLI

One of the enigmas of your novel: Victor's
repulsion at the sight of the creature he
had carefully constructed to be beautiful.
How has this happened? How has long-
desired animation transformed beauty
into ugliness? More than mere ugliness—
into horrifying monstrousness? *How can
I describe my emotions at this catastrophe?*
Had you experienced this emotion too?
The imagined baby, long in your womb,
versus the writhing thing that emerged
from your labor? A thing that could kill you,
as you had your mother? Then there was
the terrifying prospect of keeping it alive.

Transformation

XLII

It is only when Victor is on the verge of
bringing to life a female creature that
he imagines the scale of devilry and
devastation his creations would be
capable of wreaking. He violently dis-
assembles her and disappears her
still-dead parts into the deepest sea.
Sinking, they make *a gurgling sound.*
Was this your sense? That the female
conjures the worst version of a man?
One that mistreats, undervalues, and
exploits for the satisfaction of his delicate
ego? Were you always waiting for dis-
assembly and disposal in the depthless sea?

Disassembly

XLIII

We've lost sight of one of your ambitons:
to enter the conversation, the vitalist debate.
What is the enigmatic life force, something
like electricity or more divine in origin?
Then there were the cases of the feral
children, the Wild Boys and Girls. Were
they *Homo sapiens* or some other species?
These were headline-grabbing current affairs.
Your book would comment on these topics,
enliven the discourse dramatically, even if,
at first, you were unable to speak in your
own forceful, feminine voice. Readers
assumed the anonymous author was a man,
your husband or your father likely candidates.

Currency

XLIV

Your book, with its complex structure
and incredible scenarios, expresses
a deep-seated fear felt by every author.
What if, after all this fussing and fretting—
plot twists, character traits, word choices—
all this sacrificed time—no one reads it?
Margaret Saville, the intended audience,
is, after all, thousands of miles away.
You knew better than most the potential
power of a well-wrought book—your mother's,
your father's, Shelley's—but you also were
aware that a book was like a loaded
revolver: its effects, good or ill, can
only be realized when taken in hand.

Readership

XLV

We are so infatuated with the trio of
male narrators, we tend to look past
your book's females, whose perfection
prefigured the Victorian *angel in the
house*. Caroline, Elizabeth, Justine,
Agatha, Safie. Even the she-creature
represents the promise of domestic
tranquility, a return to glorious Eden.
Do they reflect your fear of domesticity?
Of being chained to the roles of wife,
mother, daughter? The angels are all
erased from the story, through death
or disappearance. Was authorship your
stratagem to escape eternal erasure?

Angel

XLVI

Shelley was dispatched to Bristol—
Fanny's letters were so despondent.
Long night of waiting. 2 A.M. and he
bore no news. One rejection after
another (including likely Shelley's)
left her in a hotel room with her
leaden heart and too much laudanum.
She said she would be easily forgotten.
Fanny died this night: your journal.
Your father wouldn't even let you
claim her body. *Disturb not the silent
dead*, he wrote. Her corpse's fate
may have been a medical student's
dissection table. If so, the tragic irony.

Silence

XLVII

You heard the news about Percy's wife
several days later: Harriet had drowned
herself in the Serpentine, Hyde Park.
Heavily pregnant, she believed she'd
been abandoned a second time—by
the soldier who'd been sent abroad
and wasn't replying to her letters. A
note addressed the care of her children.
You must have feared Harriet's fate was
foreshadowing your own. How long before
Shelley—Shelley of the wandering eye—
found a new infatuation? He so easily
abandoned his wife, unmoved by her
wretchedness, adept at self-exoneration.

Exoneration

XLVIII

We have some sense of how the suicides
affected you. Your half sister (laudanum)
then Percy's wife (laudanum and drowning)
in close succession. They must have recalled
your mother's failed attempts before your
birth, attempts by similar means. Would
you have prevented a third try, or prompted
it—had she survived your difficult arrival?
In your misery you withdrew from everyone
except your fictional characters. Did you
consider it? Did the creature with whom
you identified so closely act for you in effigy?
Soon these burning miseries will be extinct.
I shall ascend my funeral pile triumphantly.

Effigy

XLIX

Percy suggested the idea of marriage via
letter as it would make a number of people
happy—your father most of all (he desired
the benefit of your marrying well). Mainly
it may gain some favor with the court,
which was denying Percy custody of his
children by Harriet, only a month deceased.
Percy's advocate advised the hasty action.
Shelley proposed that your union would
not be barren of good. You expressed a
juvenile giddiness at the idea of your name
being Shelley. If not exactly happiness, at
least relief. Already a mother and pregnant
again in the sanctuary of St. Mildred's Church.

Proposition

L

You passed your manuscript to Percy,
the first man of many to misunderstand
what you'd achieved. You allowed him
and his Oxford education free rein. His
editorial pen was blind to the creature's
humanity and more forgiving of Victor's
flaws. And everywhere he gave your
direct style an intimidating baroqueness.
Autodidacticism led to your idiosyncratic
style. You wrote with power and plainness
and a spareness of punctuation. A fondness
for dashes (*à la* Dickinson to come). You
may have indited with a simplicity, an
honesty that you suddenly yearned for.

Edition

LI

Shelley gambled on your literary abilities—
the offspring of two authors whom he
admired. You, too, believed authorship
must surely be your destiny. But you were
unproven at sixteen. Perhaps Percy could
mold you into the intellectual partner, the
near-equal he desired (his wife, Harriet,
had turned out to be a disappointment).
As you tenaciously tackled the writing of
your book—soldiering from brief fragment
to story to full-length novel, expanding,
inserting, amending, you both delighted
in the discovery of your talent. You were
indeed worthy of the name Wollstonecraft.

Delight

LII

Your work done, you reread the Third
Canto. Already last year's frigid summer,
filled with so much worry and pain, was
inspiring a sense of nostalgia. Already at
nineteen you knew it was a special time
that would never be again. Each passage
of *Childe Harold* evoked a vivid memory
but one that would fade through the years.
This summer too, you knew, searching
for a publisher (and finding one, surely)
would become a kind of fond keepsake
in your memory, a decaying treasure over
time. Shelley and you shepherding the
book while you recalled Byron fondly.

Keepsake

LIII

How did you feel about your book?
Simple relief at having finished it?
A source of much-needed income?
Fulfillment of your literary destiny?
Did you see all the parallels between
your life and your book, all the multi-
faceted doppelgangers? Some, of
course—they were deliberate—but all?
By the end your sympathy lay with
the unnamed creature, as anonymous
as your book would be, and as open
to competing interpretations: a thing
equal parts projection and reflection,
for any reader brave enough to gaze.

Interpretation

LIV

We think of your struggles: motherhood,
bereavement, family dynamics, your
father's cold shoulder, Shelley's shifting
interests. The crises, the dramas. Ever-
present pecuniary woes. We think of
your soldiering through your first novel.
We think of your Herculean feats of
reading and the acquisition of languages.
But you had your pleasant pastimes too.
Playing chess (often with Hogg, who
admired you). Making art (you took
lessons). Gardening (the home in Marlow
afforded you space). We should remember
you always remained open to simple joys.

Joy

LV

Your industry, your tenacity amaze us.
When the proofs of your book arrived,
you did your best, but you were exhausted
and *surrounded by babes*: Claire's (and
Byron's) Allegra, William, and the newly
born Clara for whom you struggled to
produce enough milk. Percy and Claire
were nearly as needful as the infants.
Amid this Circus Maximus you'd written
two books. The *History* of your 1814
elopement was published in December,
anonymously. Readers' positive response
must've been a relief—a good omen for
the novel about to change everything.

Omen

LVI

Before any reviews were penned, your
circle praised your book and what you'd
achieved. Your father, who'd been so
distant, bragged it was the best book
written by a twenty-year-old he knew of.
Byron: *a wonderful work* (qualifying) *for
a Girl not nineteen.* Claire: *full of genius*
(showing) *a strong and cultivated intellect.*
The month before your book's release
you were busy preparing for Italy. You
shopped. You carefully packed a hundred
books to send ahead. You closed the Marlow
house. You may have felt almost carefree—
blissfully ignorant of what was to come.

Bliss

LVII

It's no wonder pregnancy was on your
mind—yours, Claire's, Harriet's—imposing
itself on your creative process. It requires
Walton nine months to assemble Victor's
story into a coherent narrative. 276 days.
You required nine months to assemble
your initial notes and sketches into the
manuscript, with its trimesterly structure.
Perhaps it is no wonder, then, that you
absconded to the Continent just at the
book's birth and public viewing. If it be
stillborn, distancing that pain was under-
standable. Your cherished babe could die
quietly on bookshelves throughout the city.

Gestation

LVIII

March 1818, your book's official release.
It's shocking and many of the reviews are
harsh: *a tissue of horrible and disgusting
absurdity . the present dunghill's foulest
toadstool . you must possess a diseased
imagination . you're as mad as your hero.*
But Walter Scott saw your *original genius
exciting new reflections in forcible English.*
You read none of them at the time. You all
had departed for Italy—for Percy's health—
and would have no knowledge of your
book's reception for many months. You
may not even have given it much thought
surrounded as you were by responsibilities.

Reception

LIX

We can see Jura and Mont Blanc & the
whole scene reminds me of Geneva.
You'd landed in Calais and were en route
to Lyons, eschewing Paris. The scenery
was spectacular, the weather delightful.
Then approaching the Alps *snows began*
to encroach upon the road. You entered
Italy via the treacherous Cenis Pass.
The cold foreshadowed Byron's icy
reception. You all wanted to reprise
the summer of 1816—all except the
Lord, who vowed to never see Claire
again, the mother of his daughter,
whom she'd brought, hoping, to Milan.

Reprisal

LX

In your book, God only exists as a
fictional construct, and Milton was
both architect and engineer. The
creature sees himself reflected in
Adam and in Satan—both a Chosen
One and a Cursed One. Victor, then,
plays the part of God, and he is a
flawed being, anything but supreme.
In your trials, you thought not to
apply to God's beneficence because
He was a thin fiction, strictly literary
in substance. You—both chosen and
cursed—weathered life's tempests
never waiting for divine intervention.

Fiction

LXI

Victor has embarked on a noble act,
a heroic act even: to conquer disease
and overcome the ravages of age.
To achieve victory over Death! But
it is so unnatural, so contrary to the
day's established practices, he must
carry out his experiments in secret,
collect his specimens in darkness.
You, too, must pursue your noble
calling out of public view. A woman
novelist—how unnatural, how contrary
to your times. Like Austen, Edgeworth,
Radcliffe, Burney, you must publish
your book in the darkness of anonymity.

Secrets

LXII

Elizabeth's death on her wedding night—
on her bridal bed no less—killed by Victor's
monster, must have been rife with meaning
even for your pre-Freudian audience.
Between pregnancy-related mortality and
barely understood venereal diseases, how
could women, especially, not associate sex
with deranged monstrosity and death?
Young, pretty, clever, the daughter of
infamy, you had your choice of partners:
Hogg, Polidori, Byron, no doubt others.
You selected and remained faithful to
the man sheathed in poetry, which perhaps
lent the act an air of purity, even piety.

Sex

LXIII

Revolution is necessary, the overturning
of established thought. It's what keeps
society forever clawing forward. But it
always comes at a cost. The French
Revolution was a recent illustration.
Your book's narrators, each paid a
steep price for pushing boundaries,
for pursuing the dangerous new.
You inherited that revolutionary spirit
and had grown up in the glow of your
forward-fighting mother's iconography.
You aspired to be a woman of letters
when your highest aspirations should
have been the roles of wife and mother.

Spirit

LXIV

Knowledge of classical languages was
for men, the fruit of formal education—
so your study of Latin and Greek was
itself a radical act. Plato, we believe,
affected your thinking. The nested
dialogues of the *Symposium* may be
reflected in your book's trio of frames.
And platonic yearnings are throughout.
We focus on Shelley's influence on you
and your book—but what of the reverse?
Two months after you finished your work
Percy began translating the *Symposium*,
an influential translation which reached
its final form under your editorial hand.

Dialogue

LXV

You had at last found a place in Italy
to your mutual liking: the peacefully
wooded Casa Bertini, surrounded by
mountains. You even had a garden.
But to placate Byron, which was to
placate Claire, Shelley had you travel
to Este with William and Clara, not
yet one. It was the height of summer.
Clara was ill, dysentery, dehydration.
Shelley insisted: on to Padua, then
Venice. Crossing by gondola, Clara
convulsed. At an inn, she died in
your arms. Devastated, you couldn't
attend the simple service on the beach.

Summer

LXVI

The despair you felt at Clara's death
must have been intensified by your
seeming to be alone in feeling it so
profoundly. By letter, your father
criticized: only inferior people fail
to rise above such calamities. Claire
played contentedly with her little girl.
Percy preferred Claire's gayer company.
You tried, but you couldn't help blaming
Percy. The depression and the anger
prevented you from being the bed-
partner he always desired. You still
had Willmouse, three, and you had
ink and paper and books and curiosity.

Grief

LXVII

Rome, 1819. Your spirits have improved.
Two months at Byron's villa in Naples
helped dull the pain of losing little Clara.
Willmouse is a delight. He's becoming
a chatterbox, mixing English with French
with Italian. You're pregnant again. You
track your periods with crosses in the
margins of your journal. Percy is content.
Summer, 1819. A malaria outbreak is
sweeping through sultry Rome. William
falls ill. You and Claire spend sleepless
nights at his bedside. Fever. Convulsions.
Death. *Everything on earth has lost its
interest to me.* You clutch his only portrait.

Willmouse

LXVIII

You were morbidly depressed after little
William's death . . . angry, withdrawn, cold
to everyone, especially Percy. Your father's
heartless letters—berating you for your
unseemly grief and pressuring Percy for
money—always made matters worse. You
considered suicide at twenty-two, but
were saved by the new life you carried.
Also, it may have had a healing effect
when you learned that in London your
book *seems to be universally known and
read.* Even unkind reviews had set
readers ablaze with questions about
your shocking novel and its young author.

Flame

LXIX

End of summer 1819. Still deeply mourning, but your insatiably curious mind began to look outward, leaving briefly its agonizing fixation on Willmouse's death. You had an interest in Parry's expedition, his search for the northwest passage. You'd had a fascination with polar exploration since your time in Scotland, a decade earlier. Like the stalwart crews of the *Hecla* and *Griper*, you were searching for some way through the dangerous ice—the engulfing, crushing, capricious floes. A mythical path to safety and security. To happiness. Yet there remained the fear all would be lost.

Passage

LXX

As the new life grew and you awaited the birth
(with its potential for pain and calamity) you
worked heatedly on a new novel. This not the
marriage of science and fiction; rather, auto-
biography and darkly romantic fantasy—replete
with pathos. Like your other book, the plot
is a deathbed confession: the heroine's sad
fall due to her father's incestuous obsession.
You sent the manuscript to your father for
publication. Aghast, he refused and also
wouldn't return it. Yet he didn't destroy the
little novel, perhaps recognizing its literary
merit, its kinship with his own themes and
techniques. *Mathilda* would wait 139 years.

Obsession

LXXI

The baby was born in Florence, a son, as
hardy as a newborn can seem. You felt
relief and some fulfilment at being a mother
again. He was named for his father and
his birthplace. Taking no chances, he was
the first to be baptized (*à la* Pascal's wager).
You set everything else aside and focused
all your attention on little Percy's needs.
Yet you deliberately remained somewhat
aloof, afraid of too much attachment. Should
the worst happen again it would be your own
undoing. At night you watched him sleep. By
day you walked yourself to exhaustion in
a maternal effort to produce enough milk.

Milk

LXXII

It had been the three of you all along—
you, Percy and Claire—and rumors were
always swirling. They climaxed in 1821
when former servants claimed that Percy
and Claire had had a child. You were
mortified and wrote impassioned letters
proclaiming Shelley's innocence, accusing
blackmail as the rumormongers' motive.
But there had been a child whom Percy
registered as yours and his in Naples,
in 1819. You were not present to sign
the certificate. Strangers were listed as
witnesses. Elena Adelaide was handed
to foster parents; she died at 15 months.

Mystery

LXXIII

The death of Allegra—Claire and Byron's
illegitimate daughter—must have freshened
your own losses. Byron cruelly kept Allegra
separated from her mother at a convent
school. When she died at age five, she had
no recollection of Claire. Percy was always
at the center of the incessant drama, traveling
alone, plotting, writing in secret, letters, verse.
By then, 1822, you'd grown weary of the
turmoil, the maelstroms of emotion, the
machinations, the possible infidelities, the
ridicule, even via published poems. You
weren't well suited for being a radical. You
wanted stability, monogamy, even religion.

Drama

LXXIV

Claire remained a fixture in your household,
but you and your stepsister bickered daily.
It could not have helped your disposition
that Percy clearly preferred her company.
You had no proof but it was unlikely their
mutual affection was purely platonic. In
Percy's poetry she was an inspiring comet,
you a cold moon who put him to sleep.
In Pisa you met Mavrocordatos, a prince
in exile. You decided to add Greek to
your repertoire of languages and he was
eager to tutor you. The lessons in grammar,
vocabulary, conjugation—the distraction,
the attention—were just what you needed.

Lessons

LXXV

Gradually you'd come to accept that Percy
was unreliable as a partner, a provider.
You must figure a way to provide for your-
self and your child. You sought guidance
(as you always had) in your mother's
published works. You had followed her
example in more ways than you intended.
She, too, had loved unreliable men.
Now Percy fancied Jane Williams, a new
addition to the Italian circle. She and her
common-law husband Edward. Jane was a
singer; Percy bought a guitar to accompany
her (later you would learn of love poems).
You realized you were expecting again.

Acceptance

LXXVI

The house at San Terenzo sat on the beach,
and the sea seemed to reach the very door.
You all lived on the upper floor, the Williamses
and you (and Claire). Close quarters while
the winds howled off the bay and you fair-
copied Byron's *Don Juan*. The poet had
taken a place up the coast, but it was far
from the magical summer of 1816, Geneva.
The colorful Edward Trelawny had shown
Shelley plans for a schooner and he was
taken with the idea of having it built. You
felt forebodings. Was it presentiment? Or
was it simply the worries of pregnancy, as
the sea winds buffeted your uneasy dreams?

Plans

LXXVII

Fire and ice are frequent elements in your
book. In his final speech, your creature
plans to burn himself to death alone on the
pole's desolate ice. You were hardly the first
author to embrace the binaries as metaphors
for life and death, for untamable energy and
total torpor, for uncontrollable desire and
the detachment from emotion altogether.
The irony, then, that it was the latter that
saved you after a painful miscarriage. You
were hemorrhaging dangerously when Percy,
Claire and Jane immersed you in a bath
of ice to stanch the bleeding. So close to
death, you claimed not to fear it thereafter.

Immersion

LXXVIII

Percy had saved your life but your marriage
remained in question. Before, he complained
of your *languor and hysterical affections.*
Weak from blood loss and freshly trauma-
tized, you must also cope with his open
dissatisfaction. He wanted you to be
light and airy and charmed by his wit, like
Claire, like, especially, Jane Williams.
It may have been a relief when he left
for Pisa to see about the journal he and
Byron had been planning to publish. Your
relationship was at its lowest point. You
two had never been unhappier. But you
must focus on little Percy and on yourself.

Dissatisfaction

LXXIX

What did *home* mean to you—you who
were so often uprooted without your say?
You alighted in a place of contentment
from time to time: Dundee, Marlow,
Casa Bertini, Naples—but your father or
Percy or circumstance compelled you
to move elsewhere, at times tragically,
never with *your* preferences in mind.
Was your frustration reflected in your
creature, who longed for place and
permanence? In the pleasant wood,
among the De Laceys, hidden in the
jungles of South America? But no
setting of satisfaction could survive.

Roots

LXXX

You concentrated on improving your Greek
by translating classical texts, particularly
Homer, to whose characters you may have
felt a special kinship: Telemachus, the boy
abandoned as a baby by his father, only
knowing him through stories of his exploits.
Odysseus, the great wanderer from war-torn
Troy who must survive a vengeful god.
But it was perhaps Penelope with whom
you felt the closest bond: left alone by
her husband, lured from home because
of another woman's beauty. Meanwhile
the vulturous suitors were afoot. Penelope:
long-suffering, ever-clever, ever-loyal.

Translation

LXXXI

Percy always felt himself in competition
with Byron, and he believed he always
fell short. Byron had more money, more
fame, more charisma, more lovers—and
most stinging of all, Percy accepted
Byron as the better poet. Perhaps he
could best Byron in their new hobby:
sailing the lapis-blue Gulf of La Spezia.
Percy christened his new schooner *Ariel*,
the devoted sprite in *The Tempest*, a
play about shipwreck. He insisted on
modifications wanting more and more
speed—he must outpace Byron's boat.
But each made the *Ariel* less seaworthy.

Modifications

LXXXII

Your circle began seeing Percy where he
wasn't, encountering, interacting with his
doppelganger. Even Percy had spoken to
his double. He had other ghostly and
ghastly visions: a girl rising from the sea,
an image of the departed Allegra; the
Williamses, bloody and broken-boned,
warning of peril as water filled the house.
Echoing the murder of Elizabeth in your
book, Percy saw himself strangling you
in your bed. You tried to dismiss the
episodes as overactive imaginations,
but they had set everyone on edge,
especially the easily excitable Percy.

Edge

LXXXIII

Day upon day, you and Jane Williams
watched the bay at Casa Magni waiting
for the sails of the *Ariel* to announce the
return of your husbands, who were over-
due after their sojourn to Pisa to meet
the Hunts and Lord Byron. You both had
received a letter from Percy. Yours coldly
informative; Jane's warmly affectionate.
Then Leigh Hunt's letter to Percy came,
inquiring about his safe return. Hunt was
anxious due to reports of *bad weather.*
Still weak from your miscarriage, already
fearing the worst, you collapsed, dropping
the fateful page: *Then it is all over!*

Correspondence

LXXXIV

Byron: *Poor Shelley's wife rushed into*
my room at midnight, her face pale as
marble, and terror impressed on her
brow. I have seen nothing in tragedy on
the stage so powerful, so effecting as her
appearance. The vividness of her terror—
her grief and alarm—communicated itself.
My memory often returns to that scene.
You had taken hold of your emotions.
Then you and Jane traveled all day by
mail coach to reach Byron's palazzo.
Sick as you were, you needed to know.
You needed to end the *dreadful suspense.*
Yet nothing could be said with certainty.

Uncertainty

LXXXV

You returned to Casa Magni to do the
only thing to do: wait, while Trelawny and
others traveled the coast in search of news.
You may have thought of Homer. The great
wanderer had caught a glimpse of home
before a vicious wind blew him far from Ithaca.
Maybe even now Percy was tacking his way
back to you and his son, and Jane Williams.
Meanwhile Trelawny learned that corpses
had washed ashore near Livorno, too water-
logged and fish-eaten to easily identify. One
deadman carried books in his pockets, Keats
and Sophocles. The rotting bodies, ten days
in the sea, were quickly buried in the sand.

Aeolus

LXXXVI

Edward Trelawny, June 19th, 1822:
I went up the stairs, unannounced,
entered the room. I neither spoke,
nor did they question me. Mrs. Shelley's
large grey eyes were fixed on my face.
I turned away, unable to bear this horrid
silence. She exclaimed, 'Is there no hope?'
I did not answer but left the room.
You were twenty-four years old and had
already buried three of your four children.
Little Allegra gone too, only months before,
and your half-sister, Fanny, gone. Now you
must see to your husband's pitiful remains,
only hastily interred in a shallow grave.

Hopelessness

LXXXVII

The *Ariel* was foundering in the tempest
that had sent the Italian fishing boats to
safe harbors. One crew had spotted the
struggling little yacht and offered rescue,
but Percy, Edward and their teenage hand
declined to board the larger, sea-worthier
boat. The fishermen advised them to
lower their burdensome sails. They did not.
It was the final sighting of the *Ariel*.
You and Percy had argued. You felt he
was abandoning you, and threatened that
you and your child would not be there when
he returned. You would go to Lord Byron,
a threat meant to wound. He left anyway.

Reports

LXXXVIII

News of Percy Shelley's drowning slowly
reached England, and the conservative
press was unkind in their obituaries—
in essence, the outspoken atheist was
handed the horrific end he deserved.
Good riddance. But those who knew him
as a person, and not just the rebel poet,
expressed the tragedy of his untimely loss.
Byron observed, *He was the most gentle,*
most amiable, and 'least' worldly-minded
person I ever met . . . a degree of genius,
joined to a simplicity . . . I shall see nothing
like him ever again. You remained in Italy,
grieving, processing what had happened.

Remembrance

LXXXIX

You surely wondered why Percy refused
to save himself—why he wouldn't board
the Italian fishing boat. Simple pride. Had
he lashed his self-esteem to his ability as
a sailor? Terror perhaps. Unable to swim,
did remaining on the storm-tossed boat
seem safer than trying to reach the other,
with the generous yet anxious Italians?
Could it, you wonder, have been a desire
for death? He had asked Trelawny to
acquire prussic acid for him, a poison to
have on hand should his unhappiness
become unbearable . . . should his unhappy
marriage to you become unbearable.

Speculation

XC

More than a month after the drowning,
Trelawny, Byron and Leigh Hunt saw to
the cremations, using an iron container
on the lonely beach, after their grisly
remains had been exhumed. One at a
time, each required a full day of fire and
spices (to mask the nauseating odor).
Edward Williams first, then Percy.
When they opened the crematorium to
retrieve Percy's ashes, they found that
his heart had not been burned to dust.
Hunt preserved it in wine, determined
not to return it to you. Still devastated,
newly widowed, you remained in Pisa.

Remnant

XCI

In the months that followed Percy's death
you turned to your steadiest companion:
the written word. For Leigh Hunt's new
journal, *The Liberal*, you contributed
Shelley's verse translation of Goethe's
Faust; and you penned a story of your
own, *A Tale of Passions*. You continued
to assist Byron with cantos of *Don Juan*.
The most daunting undertaking, though,
was the recovery of Percy's poetry, which
was scattered across the Continent,
some published, much not—many poems
merely scribbled on scraps of paper. You
were dedicated to Shelley's image as poet.

Recovery

XCII

What was the driving force behind your
determination to collect, edit, publish and
promote Shelley's poetry? Expiation of
guilt due to the way your relationship had
ended: your final words were hurled like
javelins. Or the glibness of so many, glad
the radical blasphemer, the adulterer could
deliver no further affronts to the Almighty.
And there were the rumors, the sentiment
that your coldness and the unhappiness
it provoked prevented Shelley from being
more productive. The years spent with you
crippled his creativity. It must have worried
your peace of mind, pestered like a biting fly.

Pest

XCIII

Recovery of Shelley's work proved a
more challenging task than you may have
foreseen. The letters, the requests that
mirrored your vagabond wanderings.
Percy's careless penmanship that had
to be deciphered. Then there were his
father's impediments. He preferred his
profligate son to be forgotten entirely.
You persisted and reconstructed Percy
poem by poem—a life's work reflecting
his fearless enthusiasm, his adoration
of Nature, his kindness, his affection.
No man, you said, *was more devoted*
to making those around him happy.

Reconstruction

XCIV

Was it really Shelley's heart that survived
his white-hot cremation? Historians have
long been dubious. Whatever it was,
Trelawny burned his hand retrieving it,
and Leigh Hunt intended to keep it for
himself, denying your requests—until
Byron and Jane Williams convinced
him that Percy's widow should have it.
You kept it wrapped in silk, along with
Percy's elegy on the death of Keats,
inside a drawer of your writing desk.
Perhaps it was a macabre emblem
of the memory you were determined
to immortalize. Or a soul to cherish.

Immortality

XCV

You'd always found Lord Byron's company
pleasing—which Claire found irksome after
his rejection. But Byron respected you and
paid for your expertise: first as his fair-
copyist, then as his editor. Yours was the
final word on *Don Juan* before the cantos
were sent to the poet's English publisher.
Your literary judgment was valued highly.
And Byron wanted to be your benefactor
after Percy's death, except you found his
company unsettling. You were so used to
hearing the poets in animated conversation
that when Byron spoke you waited for your
husband's reply: a voice forever silenced.

Response

XCVI

As the shock of Percy's death subsided,
your situation became clear: you were
a young woman, a young mother without
means: a dead husband who'd fled England
to elude debt-collectors, a chronically
insolvent father, a hostile and niggardly
father-in-law. Perhaps you could support
yourself and your son via your pen.
Lackington had sold all 500 copies of
your book to shops, netting you a profit
of £41. No further income from it was
forthcoming, but its surprising notoriety
gave the *nom de plume* "By the Author
of 'Frankenstein'" a marketable cachet.

Gravitas

XCVII

1823. You and the Hunts shared a house
in Genoa. Their six children were practically
feral, their upbringing had been so liberally
laissez-faire. The bedlam combined with
the depression that dogged you made writing
difficult—yet your income depended on it.
Percy's father was pressuring you to give
up your son, to be raised in his household.
Meanwhile your book was increasing in
popularity. *It is universally known,* reported
your father, *and everywhere respected.* Your
next, *Valperga,* had come out in February
to good reviews. You decided it was time
for you and Percy Florence to go home.

Time

XCVIII

Only days after returning to London you
took in a show at the English Opera House:
Peake's adaptation of your book, titled
Presumption. You were fascinated to see
your characters brought to life, even with
all the alterations. The monster took center-
stage, as he had in your imagination. Now,
however, he was rendered inarticulate.
Still, you appreciated that he was unnamed
in the program. You likely had no sense of
what the play portended for popular culture's
understanding of your serious-minded book.
Nor how closely tied to those inaccurate
representations you would be in history.

Production

XCIX

The creature's voice bursts forth from the
center of your book. Articulate, impassioned
yet rational, advocating for himself and all
the unfairly alienated. Even still, his story
is buried beneath Victor's and Walton's.
Was it your voice, at last, bursting forth?
Your eloquence unleashed? Yet entombed
in anonymity, and mistaken for Shelley's.
It is significant—it is symbolic—that the
creature was quickly stripped of his voice
and his intelligence, 1823, and they have
remained well-kept secrets ever since.
Readers must find them, resurrect them,
as if buried in graves and charnel-houses.

Resurrection

C

The time has arrived to leave you, my friend.
I know, of course, of the remaining years—
filled with other victories, other fears—
living alongside ghosts until the end.
You recast the past to mold the present.
The new age demanded conformity:
Fitting in the only way to be free.
Radicalism's coins had all been spent.
Twenty-five winters I taught your novel.
I picture you as the adolescent girl,
in back, quiet, gray-eyed like Athena.
Your eager need for knowledge unquelled.
Quite capable of capturing the world.
All the brilliant Marys: I have seen you.

Epilogue

About the Author

Ted Morrissey has been called "the modern-day Hawthorne" (*Reader Views*), and he's been the recipient of several literary awards, including the American Fiction Award, the International Book Award, and the Manhattan Book Award; he's also been nominated for a Pushcart Prize, the Kirkus Prize, and the *Best American Mystery and Suspense* anthology. His novels include *Mrs Saville*, a sequel to Mary Shelley's *Frankenstein*; and *An Untimely Frost*, also inspired by the life and times of Mary Shelley. Retired from full-time teaching, he continues to teach online for Lindenwood University and Southern New Hampshire University. He co-hosts (with Brady Harrison and Grant Tracey) the monthly podcast *A Lesson before Writing*. In 2024-25, he had the honor of delivering by invitation a series of lectures remotely to colleagues and students in Hue, Vietnam; Islamabad, Pakistan; Kabul, Afghanistan; and Tehran, Iran. The topics included the evolution of the English language, a history of popular fiction, psychoanalytic criticism, and literary trauma theory. Like the poet Carl Sandburg, Ted was born and raised in Galesburg, Illinois.

For those who may be interested, here is the order of the sonnets' composition, which is quite different from how they appear in the collection:

Vindication - St. Pancras - Marooned - Devotion - Acolyte - Escape - Matriculation - Cold* - Myth - Intelligence* - Recitation - Gossip - Exploration - Creation - Tumult - Risk - Anemia - Separation - Companions - Terror - Alchemy - Light - Effigy - Assembly - Structure - Faith - Gestation - Edition - Introspection - Machinations - Silence - Exoneration - Proposition - Currency - Keepsake - Interpretation - Readership - Joy - Transformation - Resurrection - Absence - Arrival - Disassembly - Omen - Reception - Bliss - Reprisal - Fiction - Secrets - Sex - Spirit - Summer - Grief - Angel - Vessel - Willmouse - Flame - Passage - Sweden - Obsession - Milk - Contradiction - Drama - Lessons - Acceptance - Plans - Immersion - Dissatisfaction - Translation - Modifications - Edge - Correspondence - Uncertainty - Aeolus - Hopelessness - Reports - Remembrance - Speculation - Remnant - Recovery - Pest - Reconstruction - Gravitas - Time - Production - Epilogue - Mystery - Revision - Dissipation - Immortality - Guest - Response - Paternity* - Roots - Transport - Wolves - Hunting - Caprice - Trinity - Anticipation - Metamorphosis - Dialogue - Delight

* Sonnets omitted from the collection in its final form. A total of 103 sonnets were composed. — T. M.

www.ingramcontent.com/pod-product-compliance
Lightning Source LLC
Chambersburg PA
CBHW020452100426
42813CB00031B/3335/J